Messages & Reminders FROM D.P. Divine parent

VOLUME II

by Dr. Sherrilyn Kirchner

Balboa Press books may be ordered through booksellers or by contacting:

Balboa Press
A Division of Hay House
1663 Liberty Drive
Bloomington, IN 47403
www.balboapress.com
844-682-1282

Because of the dynamic nature of the Internet, any web addresses or links contained in this book may have changed since publication and may no longer be valid. The views expressed in this work are solely those of the author and do not necessarily reflect the views of the publisher, and the publisher hereby disclaims any responsibility for them.

Any people depicted in stock imagery provided by Storyblocks are models, and such images are being used for illustrative purposes only.
Storyblocks.com

ISBN: 979-8-7652-4423-4 (sc)
ISBN: 979-8-7652-4424-1 (hc)
ISBN: 979-8-7652-4422-7 (e)

Print information available on the last page.

Balboa Press rev. date: 08/04/2023

Dedicated to all Divine children.

— CONTENTS —

— A MESSAGE FROM DR. K. —

Welcome, Divine child. I am Dr. Sherrilyn Kirchner, a metaphysician specializing in holistic healing. In working with my clients over the years, I've noticed a common need for a completely supportive and all-accepting parental figure that can offer beneficial advice, undivided attention, complete acceptance, and unconditional love. To fill that need, I created *D.p.* (Divine parent).

D.p. is an icon that represents the ideal parental figure. The parent who supports without judgment, who loves without condition, and who guides without doubt. The most important thing to remember about D.p. is that this parent lives within you. You are never separated from D.p. — D.p. is always with you. D.p. is a part of you.

This is the second volume in the *Messages & Reminders from D.p.* series, which is designed to help you understand, embrace, and hone your Divine creative power. This work may be challenging, but it is work only you can do. You are the only one who can take control of your own evolution by implementing practices such as these. The more time you spend with the *Messages & Reminders* in this book, the more powerful you'll become. You *can* create the life you desire, but you must do your own self-work.

Live in the Body, Master the Mind, Witness through Spirit.

— Dr. K.

NOTE: Please refer to the Glossary at the end of this book to further familiarize yourself with the key concepts used throughout this series.

— INTRODUCTION —

Greetings, Divine child. I am *D.p.*, your Divine parent. I reside within the eternal Divine consciousness, which resides within you.

My ultimate purpose is to help awaken in you a renewed awareness of the immense power that lives within you by offering *Messages & Reminders* of forgotten truths. Deep down, you know of your powerful creation abilities, but because of the veil of the human experience, most of you have forgotten your true creative potential. In order to create the life you want, it is vitally important that you remember these truths and implement them into your life.

As Divine children, you have a Divine right to experience all that you desire. You are already using your Divine creative power by attracting and allowing this book into your life. Now is the time to delve further and connect to your immense power within. In this endeavor, I offer you unconditional love, support, and acceptance.

D.p.

— HOW TO BENEFIT FROM THESE MESSAGES & REMINDERS —

This book is designed to provide insight on certain self-empowering principles along with weekly practices to help you implement each principle into your daily life. The *Messages & Reminders* are organized in a progressive fashion, but if you feel called to work out of order, please follow your intuition. See what resonates with you. Regardless of how you progress through the book, know that there is no right or wrong way. Just remember that implementation is key. It's easy to understand a concept. It's much more challenging — and rewarding — to implement these concepts into your daily life.

The weekly practices encourage focus and effort. I suggest you choose a certain day of the week on which to explore each week's Message or Reminder. It may help to add a daily reminder on your calendar to keep track of which Message or Reminder you're focusing on that week, in addition to utilizing the notes section to track your experience. Ultimately, you are in charge of your life, and you decide how you want to approach and interact with this information.

I recommend you set your intentions each day and listen for your truths to emerge. *What do you want to get out of this? What changes do you want to create?* Keep a record. Write out your intentions and your newfound awareness along with any challenges and successes. It will be much easier to see your progress that way.

Remember, this work is up to you. No one else can evolve for you. You already have everything you need within you. All you have to do is make the choice to continue. Complete self-love is the key to unlock any door, and you hold this key within.

DISCLAIMER: As a metaphysician, I present these findings and suggestions through the "do no harm" lens. As with everything that is offered through Holistic Life Source, the information in this book is up to you to interpret and discern for yourself. Only do what you feel is best for you and the world you live in.

Messages & Reminders

F R O M

D.p.

ABOUT MY...

Awareness

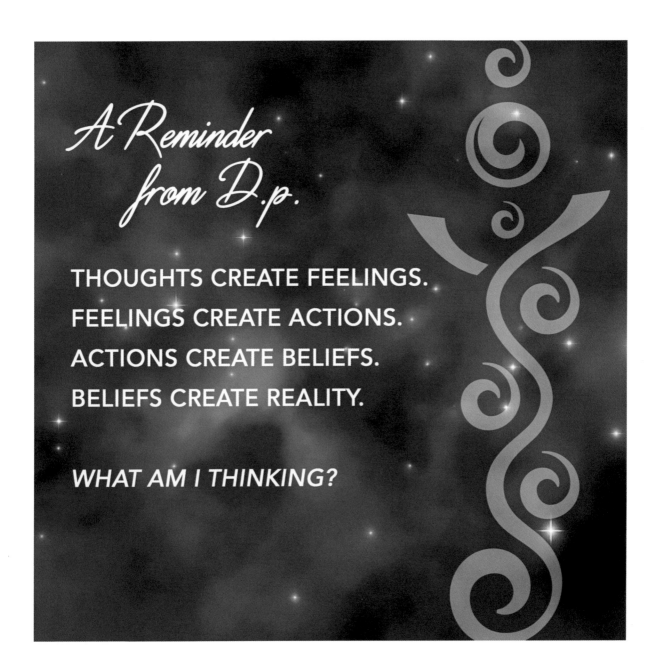

A Reminder from D.p.

THOUGHTS CREATE FEELINGS.

FEELINGS CREATE ACTIONS.

ACTIONS CREATE BELIEFS.

BELIEFS CREATE REALITY.

WHAT AM I THINKING?

14

All that is created begins with a thought, and I am creating my reality with every thought I think. As I think a thought, I have a feeling. As I have a feeling, I respond with an action or reaction. When I act or react, I form habits. These habits then form my beliefs about the world and myself, which become my belief systems. And my belief systems then create my identities, which in turn create my reality. Everything starts with a thought.

NOTE: The average person thinks tens of thousands of thoughts per day. Often, these thoughts are involuntary, redundant, and familiar. It's the mind on autopilot, churning out thousands of reality-creating thoughts that do not serve our highest good.

PRACTICE: This week, I pay close attention to my thoughts and how my thoughts make me feel. I do this by taking note of how I feel throughout my day. If I do not like how I feel, I change my thoughts, then notice how my actions or reactions change. As I continue to implement this practice, I reveal the great creative power within me. I *can* change my reality.

I must remember, even when it seems as though things aren't going my way, that I create or co-create each situation for a reason. Ego wants me to play the victim, telling me that I have no power over my circumstances, but my true-self knows that I am the creator of everything in my life. I must take responsibility for my reality and learn the lessons my manifestations have revealed. Only then will I be able to attract and allow what it is I truly desire.

PRACTICE: This week, I take a look at the parts of my life where I seem to struggle the most. Without resistance or self-judgment, I investigate these aspects of my present reality to determine why I created (or co-created) them. *What lessons do I need to learn from these experiences? How does this new awareness benefit my life?* I remember that everything is only energy. This helps me know that I can create anything I want. I am the creator of my experience and my creations exist to help me evolve.

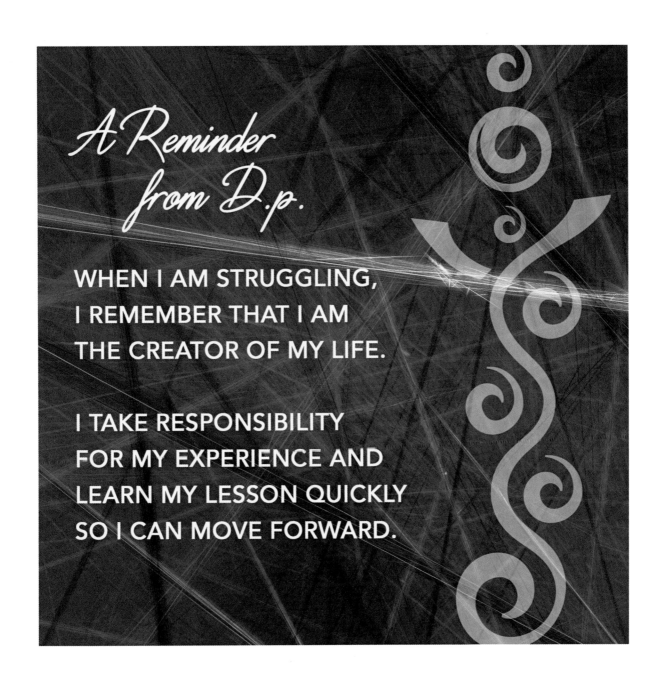

A Reminder from D.p.

WHEN I AM STRUGGLING,
I REMEMBER THAT I AM
THE CREATOR OF MY LIFE.

I TAKE RESPONSIBILITY
FOR MY EXPERIENCE AND
LEARN MY LESSON QUICKLY
SO I CAN MOVE FORWARD.

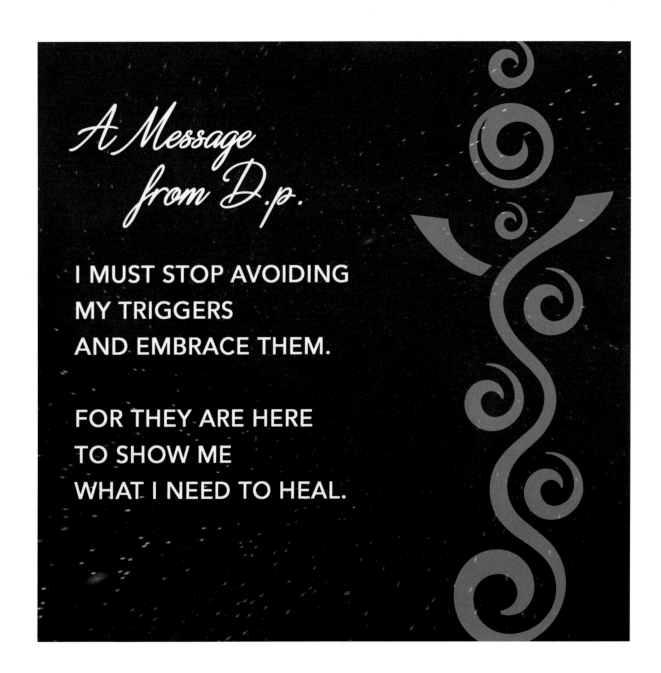

A Message from D.p.

I MUST STOP AVOIDING
MY TRIGGERS
AND EMBRACE THEM.

FOR THEY ARE HERE
TO SHOW ME
WHAT I NEED TO HEAL.

What is a trigger? A trigger can be a remark, an encounter, a conversation, a thought, or an experience of some kind. The most important element of any trigger is this: it signals an opportunity to choose between perpetuating an old pattern that does not serve me or creating a new reality.

Triggers are fear-based. They are programs created and used by the ego to prevent me from experiencing unwanted feelings. Sometimes they help me define my personal boundaries, but other times they prevent me from living the life I want. When that happens, I must remember that I have the power to free myself of them if I choose.

PRACTICE: This week, I pay close attention to my reactions. When someone says or does something that triggers an unwanted feeling, I focus on the sensation. *Is there a lump in my throat? A tightness in my chest? Do I feel like I need to cry or yell?* Whatever it is, I feel it. (The mind will try to keep me focused on my thoughts, but I know to focus on my body.) I feel it until I cannot feel it anymore. I allow the blocked energy to move, respectfully commanding the feeling to leave my body, and in so doing I raise my vibrational frequency. This is one of the most challenging practices in this book, but also one of the most integral to my evolution. This takes time and effort, but the effects are life-changing, literally.

NOTE: This practice does not need to be done in the moment; it can be done after-the-fact, when I am in a safe environment. All I have to do is recall the triggering event and then focus on the sensation that arises.

— *Notes* —

My true-self knows what's best for me — it knows what I need to do to live the life I desire. *But how well do I implement this knowledge?* I can listen to the self-help gurus and agree with their teachings, *but am I actually doing the work?*

Many of us stop at the enlightenment stage — we know our truth; we know what we need to do. But few of us continue on to the empowerment stage — putting that knowledge into practice and making it a part of our daily lives.

If I really want to change my life, enlightenment is not enough. I must also implement what I've learned; I must empower myself.

PRACTICE: This week, I identify one or two teachings I agree with — be it from this book or another source — and work to implement them into my daily life. At the end of the week, I assess: *Did this new practice resonate with me? Do I feel more empowered? Do I need to spend more time implementing it?* Remember, I can always adjust if something doesn't feel right. And my true-self always knows what's right for me.

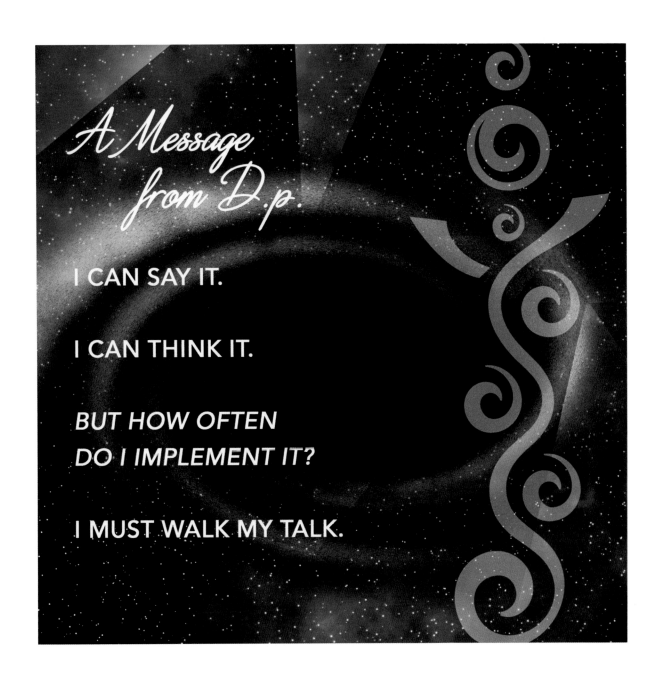

A Message from D.p.

I CAN SAY IT.

I CAN THINK IT.

BUT HOW OFTEN
DO I IMPLEMENT IT?

I MUST WALK MY TALK.

Messages & Reminders

FROM

D.p.

ABOUT MY...

Intuition

A Message from D.p.

GET STILL.

BE PRESENT.

BREATHE.

LISTEN FOR
MY TRUTH.

If I am constantly talking about, thinking about, watching, or distracted by external events, *how will I be able to hear my inner-voice? My truth?*

Only when I am in a state of stillness can I truly hear my inner-voice. Stillness does not mean isolation. Nor does it mean silence. I can achieve stillness anywhere at any time, but it takes practice. The more I practice listening to my truth — paying attention to how my body reacts to different stimuli and noticing when I am in and out of energetic alignment — the easier it will be to reach a level of stillness in any environment.

PRACTICE: This week, I focus on listening to my inner-voice by staying in the present moment and monitoring the sensations in my body. I do not force stillness; I take a breath, relax, and allow it.

— *Notes* —

How often do I listen to my intuition, my inner-voice? Even with small things, like the feeling that I should turn left instead of right. *Do I listen?*

The more I listen to my intuition, the more I trust myself — my true-self. Gaining trust in myself is one of the most empowering practices, for it puts me in harmony with my truth. When I trust my intuition, I strengthen my alignment to my highest good. This helps me avoid unwanted experiences, protect my boundaries, and heal.

PRACTICE: This week, I practice honing my intuitive abilities by listening within. As I go through my day, I listen for my inner-voice. When I hear it, I follow the instructions. The more I do this, the better I will become at discerning my ego-mind from my true-self.

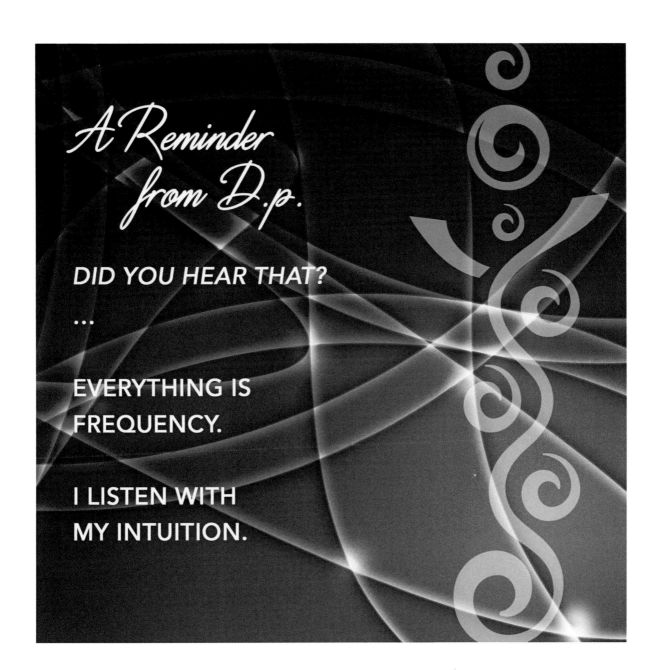

A Reminder from D.p.

DID YOU HEAR THAT?

...

EVERYTHING IS
FREQUENCY.

I LISTEN WITH
MY INTUITION.

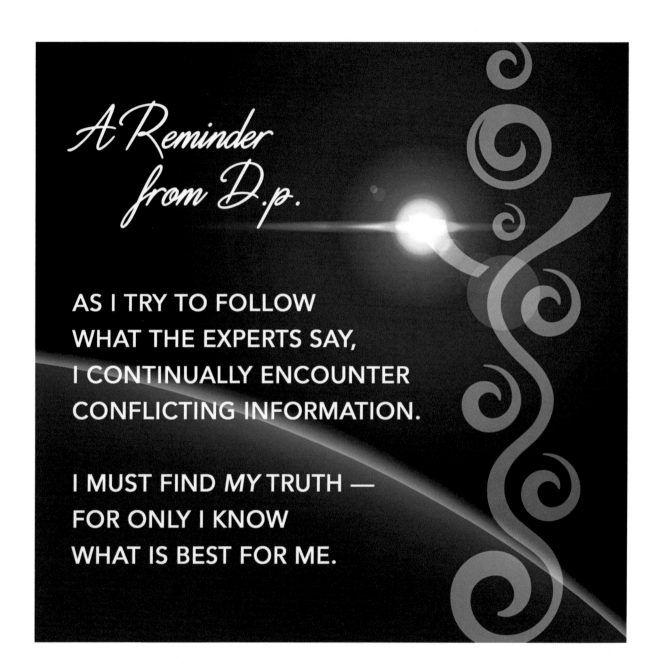

A Reminder from D.p.

AS I TRY TO FOLLOW
WHAT THE EXPERTS SAY,
I CONTINUALLY ENCOUNTER
CONFLICTING INFORMATION.

I MUST FIND *MY* TRUTH —
FOR ONLY I KNOW
WHAT IS BEST FOR ME.

How many times have I been told one piece of advice by a so-called expert and then a conflicting piece of advice by another so-called expert?

When I hear advice from the so-called experts, I give myself permission to discern whose advice, if anyone's, resonates with me. I must decide for myself what is best for me. I create my life through my beliefs and therefore have the right to choose what I believe.

I remember that only I can know what is best for me at any given time, and that what is best for me may change as my life changes. I allow myself to change my mind. Change is what helps me evolve.

PRACTICE: This week, I let myself question something I have been taught that I do not feel resonates with me. I listen to my intuition to decide whether or not I agree with this teaching, for my intuition is the voice of my true-self. I give myself the power to choose what is best for me, keeping in mind that my beliefs create my reality. *What do I want to believe about my health, my finances, my relationships, my career, and so on?*

When I ask others for their advice or opinions about my life, I allow them to add their energy to my experience. It's okay to confide in others and to ask those I trust for guidance and support, but I must remember that ultimately, my decisions are up to me.

Sometimes, listening to others too much can prevent me from hearing my own truth. Deep within myself, I already know my truth; I just have to listen to it. Others can serve as roadblocks or catalysts on my journey, but none of them know my truth. Only I know what is truly best for me.

PRACTICE: This week, I practice listening to my true-self by refraining from asking others' opinions or advice. I work on hearing my own inner guidance by sitting with myself and observing how I feel. As I do this, I gain clarity on what it is I want and don't want, which will ultimately help me create the life I truly desire.

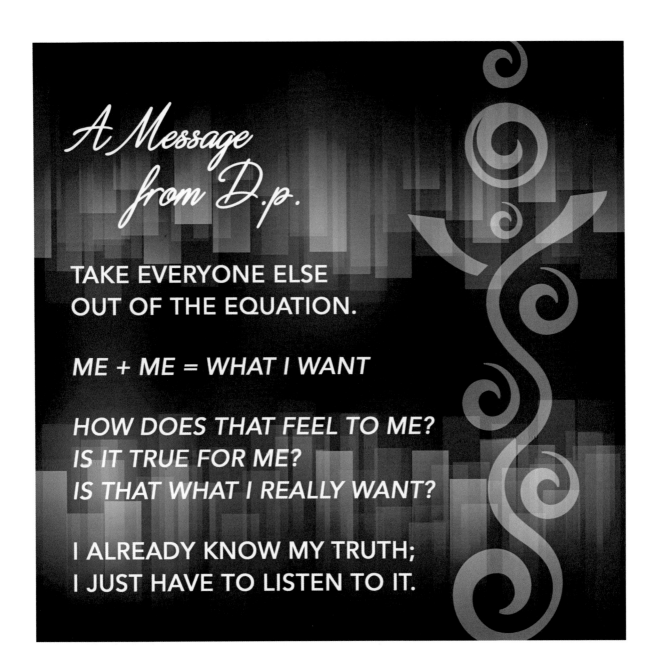

A Message from D.p.

TAKE EVERYONE ELSE
OUT OF THE EQUATION.

ME + ME = WHAT I WANT

HOW DOES THAT FEEL TO ME?
IS IT TRUE FOR ME?
IS THAT WHAT I REALLY WANT?

I ALREADY KNOW MY TRUTH;
I JUST HAVE TO LISTEN TO IT.

Messages & Reminders

F R O M

D.p.

ABOUT MY...

Truth

A Reminder from D.p.

I ACCEPT

MY TRUTH

BECAUSE

IT'S WHAT

MAKES ME

ME.

To create the life I want, I must accept all of myself, all that is me, including the aspects of myself that I want to change or hide. *What am I denying about myself? What do I not want to accept?* When I answer these questions honestly, I reclaim my creative power, the power I need to create the life I want. Accepting my truth is not about judging myself; it's about embracing what makes me unique.

PRACTICE: To reclaim my power by accepting all that I am, I take this week to embrace one of my unique traits. When I notice this trait revealing itself, I take a moment to recognize it as an essential part of me in this now moment and lean into its beauty.

— Notes —

I understand that only I need to approve of me. There is no need for anyone else to approve of my thoughts, words, and actions, for that does not serve my highest good.

When I live my life in the constant pursuit of others' approval, I cause great conflict and disharmony within myself. Trying to convince others or prove to them that I am worthy weakens my creative powers. It doesn't matter what they think of me. It only matters what I believe.

Furthermore, when I search for someone's approval, I make them an object; a dispensary of either reward or punishment. This can damage the relationship I have with that person, for they are not an object; they are a Divine creator, just like me.

PRACTICE: This week, I ask myself: *Whose approval am I seeking?* When I answer honestly, I am already beginning to reclaim my power. Being honest with myself is vital. Then comes the decision to either continue this pattern of seeking approval, or to break the pattern and create a new experience.

No one has to agree with me, and no one has to approve of me. If I believe that what I am saying and doing is what is best for me, then it becomes my truth.

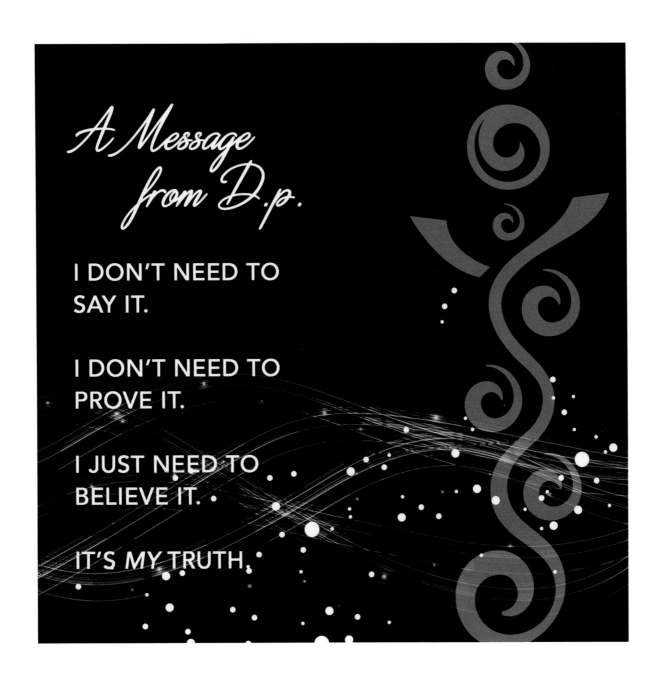

A Message from D.p.

I DON'T NEED TO SAY IT.

I DON'T NEED TO PROVE IT.

I JUST NEED TO BELIEVE IT.

IT'S MY TRUTH.

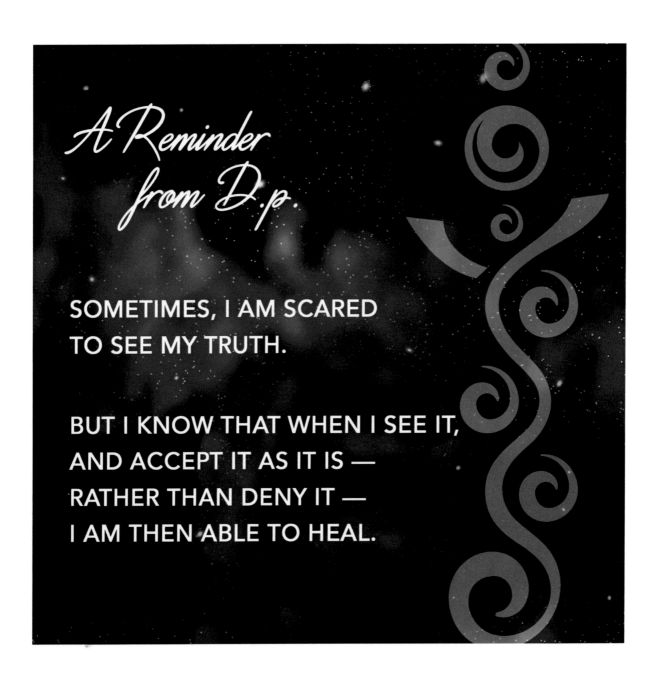

A Reminder from D.p.

SOMETIMES, I AM SCARED
TO SEE MY TRUTH.

BUT I KNOW THAT WHEN I SEE IT,
AND ACCEPT IT AS IT IS —
RATHER THAN DENY IT —
I AM THEN ABLE TO HEAL.

As I do my self-reflection work and uncover new truths, I may become aware of certain truths that cause me discomfort. These truths can create feelings of lack, loss, shame, or fear. This is perfectly natural. It signifies the movement of energy — buried emotions that are now coming to the surface to be felt, released, and healed.

If I do not admit these truths to myself, I will continue to carry them with me, and my vibrational frequency will be out of harmony, which can keep me from evolving and even cause disease.

PRACTICE: This week, I admit one truth I have been denying, repressing, or minimizing. I allow myself to see and accept this truth clearly, without judgment. I don't have to share this truth with anyone but myself, but I must own it, and own it completely. Once I do this, I can finally release the blocked energy that has been keeping me stuck and begin to heal.

When I lie, I create disharmony within my body, which can cause disease. Therefore, it is essential for my health that I tell the truth as long as it is safe to do so. Telling my truth gives me the power to manifest what I desire.

Telling the truth doesn't mean speaking without filters or spewing opinions that may hurt someone's feelings — it's about living with integrity. That means not telling lies, not making empty promises, and not pretending to be something I am not.

NOTE: Multiple studies have shown that when a person tells fewer lies, their physical health improves.

PRACTICE: This week, I practice staying aware of what I say to others, noting whether or not I feel what I say is in alignment with my truth. I listen to how I make promises, how well I follow through, and if I keep my word. I notice if I am pretending to be something I am not, and do my best to break these patterns so I am more aligned with my truth.

A Reminder from D.p.

STOP LYING.

TELL THE TRUTH —
MY TRUTH
(WITHOUT HURTING OTHERS).

MY HEALTH DEPENDS ON IT.

A Reminder from D.p.

WHY IS IT THAT
WHAT I RESIST PERSISTS?

BECAUSE NO MATTER
HOW HARD I TRY
TO REPRESS OR DENY MY TRUTH
IT IS STILL MY TRUTH.

MY TRUTH IS VIBRATIONAL.
TO REWRITE IT, I MUST ACCEPT IT.

Why do I keep reliving the same thing over and over again? Because I am a vibrational being. As I vibrate out into the universe a specific frequency, I attract that same frequency to me, encountering it through my experiences.

The laws of the universe are at work all the time. They do not punish, and they do not judge. They just are. It is up to me to change the frequency I'm sending out, if I so choose. Only then will I be able to create a new reality.

PRACTICE: This week, I focus on the patterns in my life that do not serve me. When I identify these patterns, I give myself the time I need to feel through the associated emotions (the frequencies I keep attracting), like frustration, anger, sadness, etc. When I allow myself to feel my true feelings (my sensations), I can finally release them, and in so doing, begin to create a new reality full of peace, joy, and love.

 — *Notes* —

Messages & Reminders

FROM

D.p.

ABOUT MY...

Beliefs

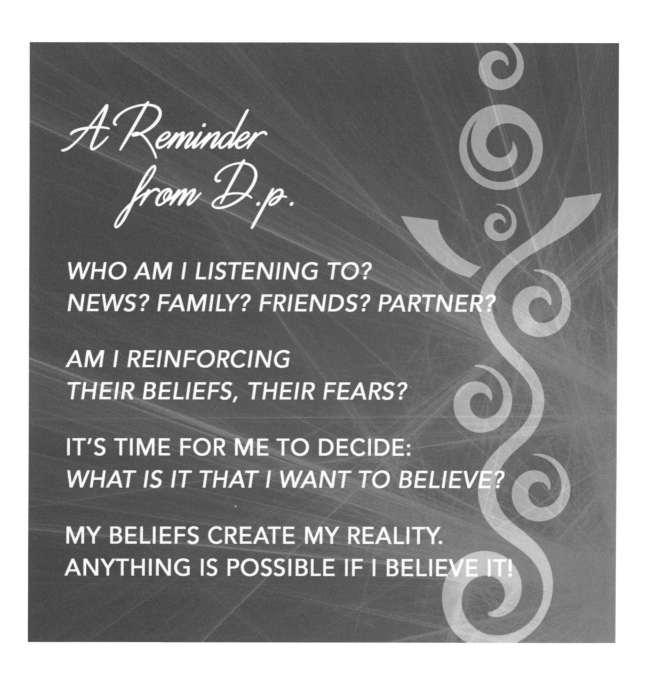

*A Reminder
from D.p.*

WHO AM I LISTENING TO?
NEWS? FAMILY? FRIENDS? PARTNER?

AM I REINFORCING
THEIR BELIEFS, THEIR FEARS?

IT'S TIME FOR ME TO DECIDE:
WHAT IS IT THAT I WANT TO BELIEVE?

MY BELIEFS CREATE MY REALITY.
ANYTHING IS POSSIBLE IF I BELIEVE IT!

I know my beliefs create my reality. So, instead of listening to others and their fear-based beliefs, I now choose to listen to my true-self. Because when I embrace beliefs that align with my true-self, I change my reality for my highest good.

I can rewire any belief I want at any time. But first I must take inventory and decide which beliefs serve my mission of self-evolution. Then I can rewire the rest.

PRACTICE: This week, I identify a belief I do not wish to hold any longer. This belief may have been passed down to me from my caregivers, or it could be a societal belief I have been conditioned to hold. Whatever the case may be, if this belief does not resonate with my true-self, I allow myself to rewrite or recalibrate it so that I can attract the reality I desire.

— Notes —

Because the *Law of Attraction* (LOA) is always working, I know that I attract into my life what I vibrate out. Therefore, when I feel judged by another, it is really because I am resonating out the frequency of self-judgment; I am allowing my ego to judge me.

I know that my ego is a master of games and deception. But I remember that I am more powerful. I can pull myself out of the game of judgment any time I want. I do this by accepting myself — every part of me.

PRACTICE: This week, I pay close attention to how I believe others are judging me. I remember that when I feel judged — which is only a reflection of a frequency that I am vibrating out — I can rewrite my ego game as I so choose. I do this by reminding myself that I am just role-playing what my ego has downloaded for survival purposes, while the real truth is that I am a perfect being and I have the Divine right to be here as my true-self.

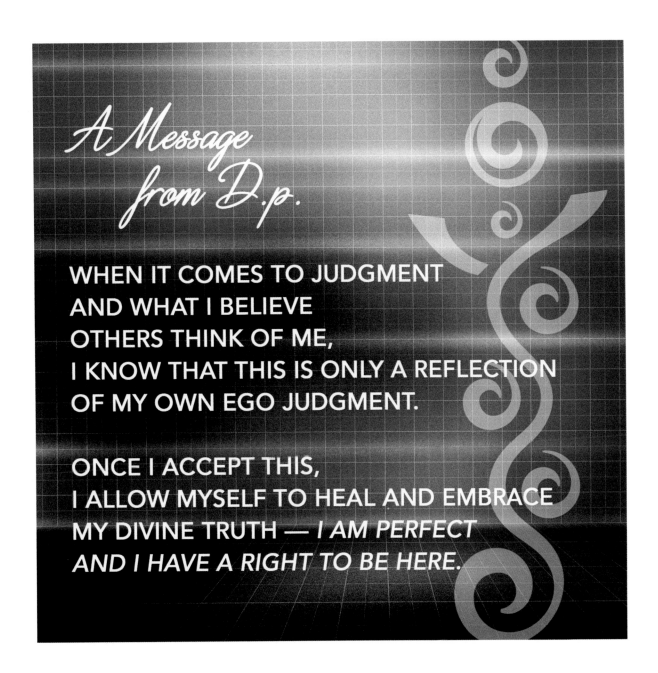

A Message from D.p.

WHEN IT COMES TO JUDGMENT
AND WHAT I BELIEVE
OTHERS THINK OF ME,
I KNOW THAT THIS IS ONLY A REFLECTION
OF MY OWN EGO JUDGMENT.

ONCE I ACCEPT THIS,
I ALLOW MYSELF TO HEAL AND EMBRACE
MY DIVINE TRUTH — *I AM PERFECT*
AND I HAVE A RIGHT TO BE HERE.

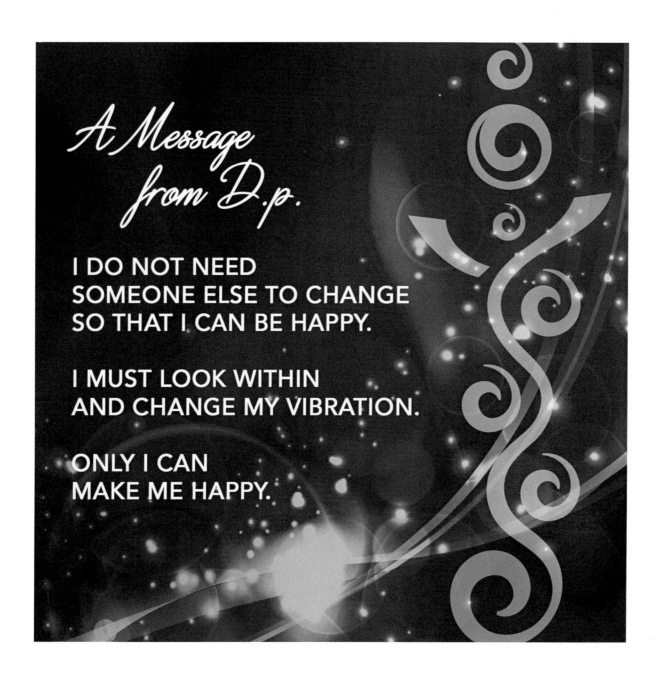

A Message from D.p.

I DO NOT NEED
SOMEONE ELSE TO CHANGE
SO THAT I CAN BE HAPPY.

I MUST LOOK WITHIN
AND CHANGE MY VIBRATION.

ONLY I CAN
MAKE ME HAPPY.

Trying to make others act the way I want them to can be a massive drain on my energy. I must remember that everyone has the right to free will, including me. If I expect someone else to be responsible for my happiness, I will be sorely disappointed. No one else can truly make me happy; only I can.

It's when I focus my energy within — aligning my thoughts, words, actions, and beliefs with my true-self — that my reality changes. My emotional state is up to me, nobody else. As I continue to implement these practices of focusing within, setting boundaries, and accepting myself, it will become easier to remain in whatever emotional state I choose, regardless of the happenings around me.

PRACTICE: This week, I focus on what I can do to create more happiness within my own life, despite what others do or say (or don't do or say). *What is it that I want or need in order to maintain a state of happiness?*

When I compete with others, in any way, I attract more competition. This is because the *Law of Attraction* (LOA) is always working. If I resonate out a vibration of challenge and competition, I create more of the same.

When I feel the need to compete or compare, I express a belief in lack. Lack is the idea that there is not enough to go around — not enough money, not enough recognition, not enough love or acceptance. This is untrue. Everything is energy, and energy is infinite. There is always enough to go around. But if I believe there isn't, I will experience lack, and feel the need to battle for what I want.

PRACTICE: This week, I ask myself: *In what areas of my life am I competing with others?* This can be competing for attention, for money, for success, for love. I remind myself that there is no need to compete. When I believe that I am worthy of all that I want, I will manifest my desires with joy and ease.

A Message
from D.p.

WHEN I STOP COMPETING

WITH OTHERS,

I AM FREE TO LIVE

MY BEST LIFE.

Messages & Reminders

FROM

D.p.

ABOUT MY...

Relationships

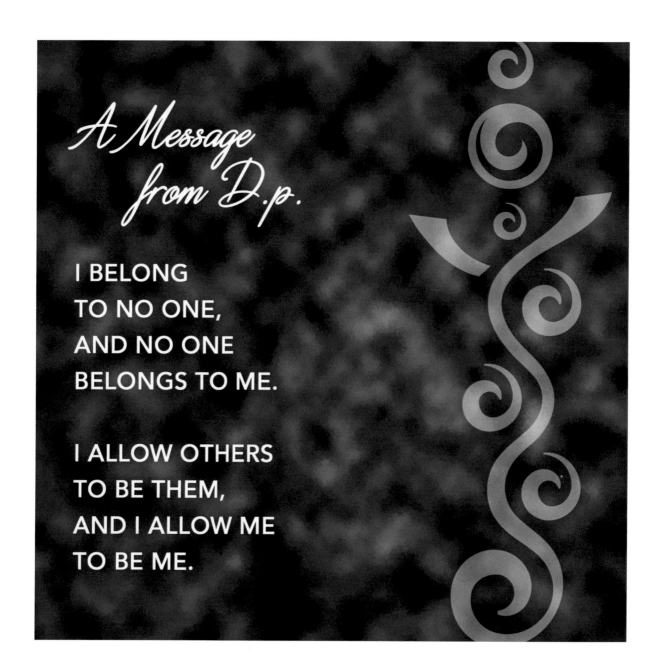

A Message from D.p.

I BELONG
TO NO ONE,
AND NO ONE
BELONGS TO ME.

I ALLOW OTHERS
TO BE THEM,
AND I ALLOW ME
TO BE ME.

I do not need to belong to anyone — and I do not need others to belong to me — to be all that I want to be. Every human is a Divine creator. The only person that matters on my journey of self-evolution is me. I already have all I need within me.

PRACTICE: This week, I notice what — and whom — I am clinging to. *Are there familiar things or people I am trying too hard to keep?* I must be honest with myself. If I feel that I am holding on too tightly, I allow myself to let go. I let go of others' behaviors and beliefs by focusing on my own behaviors and beliefs. I remind myself that everyone else can do and be and have all that they want, just like me. I have everything I need to create the life I desire.

Letting go of my desires — or my efforts — to control others' behaviors frees up my energy for greater endeavors. I know that I cannot truly control what others do; all humans have the Divine right to free will, including me.

I can always be me, regardless of anyone else's behavior. I have great power, and I am capable of changing my focus whenever I choose to do so.

PRACTICE: For this week, I pay less attention to what others are doing and focus instead on my own experiences. *What is best for me in this moment?* When I take others out of the equation, I can finally see that I am here to do what I feel is best for me so that I can live the life I desire.

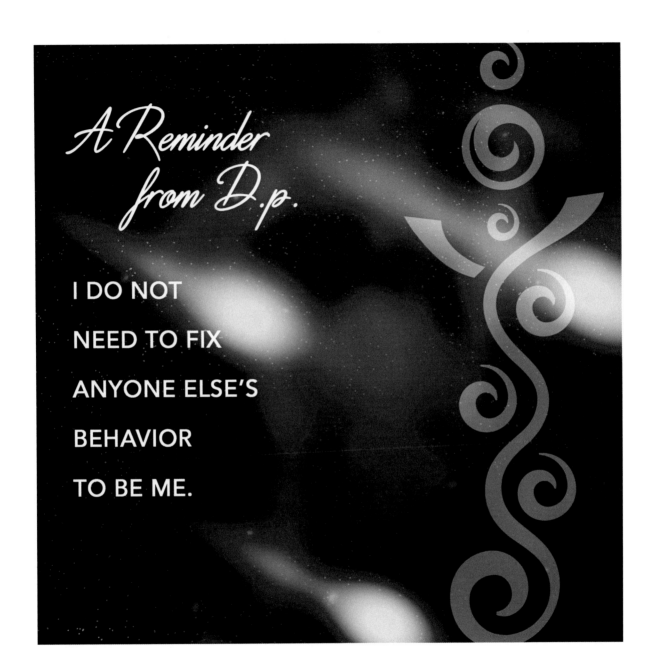

A Reminder from D.p.

I DO NOT

NEED TO FIX

ANYONE ELSE'S

BEHAVIOR

TO BE ME.

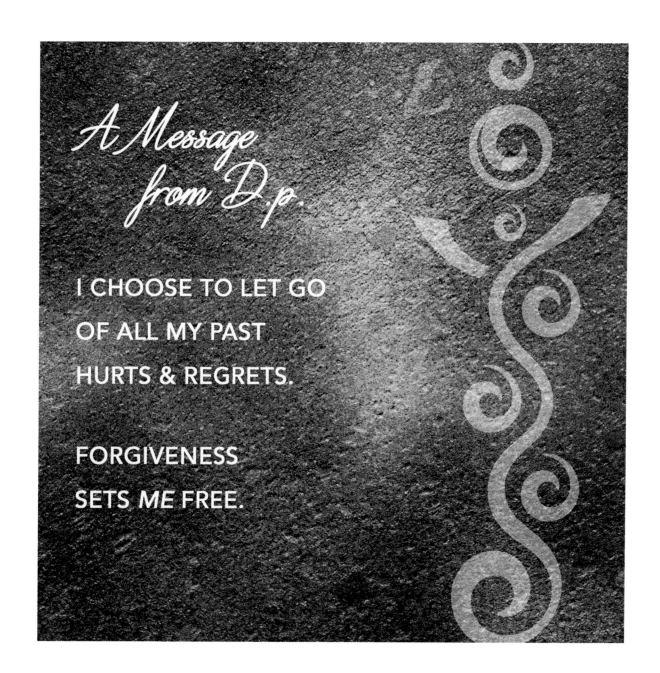

*A Message
from D.p.*

I CHOOSE TO LET GO
OF ALL MY PAST
HURTS & REGRETS.

FORGIVENESS
SETS ME FREE.

I am capable of forgiving myself and others. I am capable of letting go of any energy that does not serve me. All I need to do is choose to do so.

I remember that "mistakes" are just opportunities to learn lessons that will ultimately help me evolve. I also remember that because I create my life through my vibrational frequencies, I co-created those past experiences in part because I wished to learn the lessons they taught me. But now, I can move on. If these energies no longer serve me, I let them go.

When I let go of my past hurts and regrets, I set myself free from those lower vibrations and focus instead on creating the life I wish to live, now empowered by the lessons I've learned from those experiences.

PRACTICE: This week, I take stock of how much time and energy I spend ruminating on past hurts or regrets. When I am ready to forgive and let go of these heavy vibrational frequencies, I first acknowledge and accept that they happened. Then I send love to these experiences, gather what lessons I learned from them, and let them go once and for all.

How many times have I been criticized for feeling a certain way? "You're overreacting, settle down, just get over it." Others may think I should feel a certain way about a given situation, but it is not up to them to decide how I should feel. My feelings are my feelings — whatever they may be.

I know that my feelings are my body's way of communicating my truth to me, and that "negative" sensations are evidence of disharmony within my energetic frequency. My feelings are not good or bad, right or wrong. They are more like status reports. *How aligned am I with my true-self?*

PRACTICE: This week, I pay attention to my feelings and the associated sensations in my body. I do this as honestly as I can, letting myself feel what I feel and refraining from judging the feeling. Judging my feelings is ego-thinking, and it gets me nowhere.

I focus on feeling the feeling. *Do I feel hurt? Hopeless? Scared? Excited? Alone? Angry? Compassionate?* I validate my feelings by giving value to them; they help me see my truth. Do I notice any area of my body that feels *tight, heavy, hot, cold, pain, etc.?* If so, I focus on the sensation. This is the key to changing my frequency — this is how I change my reality.

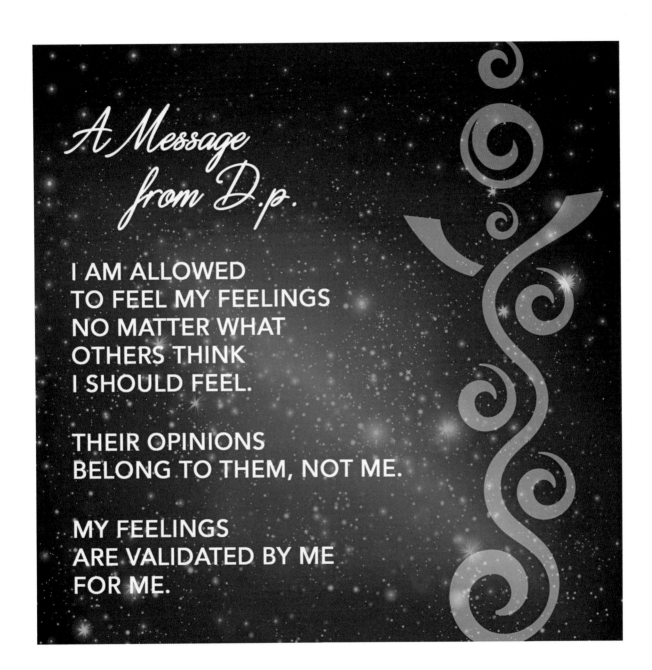

A Message
from D.p.

I AM ALLOWED
TO FEEL MY FEELINGS
NO MATTER WHAT
OTHERS THINK
I SHOULD FEEL.

THEIR OPINIONS
BELONG TO THEM, NOT ME.

MY FEELINGS
ARE VALIDATED BY ME
FOR ME.

A Reminder from D.p.

EVEN IF IT SEEMS LIKE
D.P. HAS LEFT ME,
I AM NEVER ALONE.

I AM CONNECTED TO
THE ALL — THE DIVINE ENERGY.

I AM ALWAYS AND
FOREVER CONNECTED.

Although sometimes it may seem like I am completely alone, I know that I am never truly alone. I am part of the eternal Divine family, a family that transcends the limits of space and time. D.p. is also a part of this family, for D.p. resides within me. D.p. is always with me.

I am never alone, for I am a Divine being made of the highest vibrational frequency: love. Just like everyone and everything, I am part of the All, and I am eternally loved.

PRACTICE: This week, I remember that my eternal Divine family has always been and will always be with me. I can open a channel of communication with my Divine family by practicing my intuitive listening skills. I may hear more clearly when I am out in nature, or meditating, or dreaming. My Divine family is always available to me; all I have to do is listen for them.

— Notes —

Messages & Reminders

F R O M

D.p.

ABOUT MY...

Creations

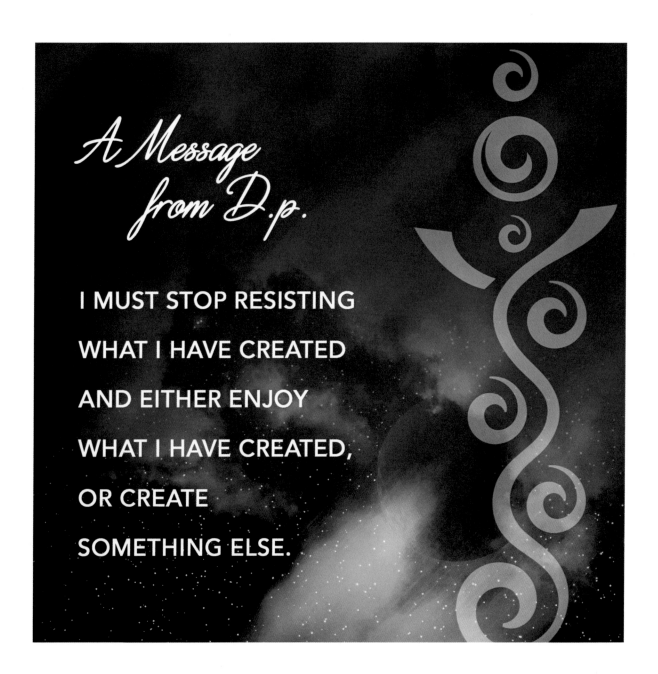

A Message from D.p.

I MUST STOP RESISTING WHAT I HAVE CREATED AND EITHER ENJOY WHAT I HAVE CREATED, OR CREATE SOMETHING ELSE.

Everything I resist is something I have created, because everything I experience is my own creation. The *Universal Law of Attraction* (LOA) states that like vibration attracts like vibration. Each vibration, each frequency I resonate out — whether low vibration or high vibration — attracts similar vibrations to me. That's how I create my reality. LOA is always working.

If I do not enjoy what I have created in my life thus far, I remember that I have the power to change my reality by changing my frequency. To do that, I first focus on my body, the keeper of my truth. I identify the sensations I do not wish to feel anymore, and I focus on them. I give them the time and attention they need to be released. If I continue to resist these uncomfortable sensations, they will continue to hold me back. In order to truly change my frequency, I must take responsibility for all my creations, and then spend the necessary time feeling through the associated sensations.

PRACTICE: This week, I stop resisting my unwanted creations. Instead, I set my intention to release these old patterns and beliefs by owning and feeling the associated sensations until the intensity lessens. If the sensation moves, I follow it. I remain with the sensation until I do not feel it anymore. This will take time and practice, but I know it is worth it, for it will literally change my reality.

A catalyst is something that pushes me to move in a different direction. It usually comes in the form of some unwanted discomfort, sometimes minor, sometimes major. But when it arrives, I understand it is for my highest good. Perhaps I've been spending too much time in my current comfort zone, or trapped in a loop of mindless distractions. The catalyst is meant to realign me with my path toward self-evolution.

PRACTICE: This week, I ask myself if there is anything in my life that is nudging me toward a new direction. *In what areas am I frustrated or unsatisfied? Have there been any recent events that have knocked me off balance?* If something comes to mind, I practice listening to my intuition. *What purpose does this catalyst serve on my path to self-evolution?*

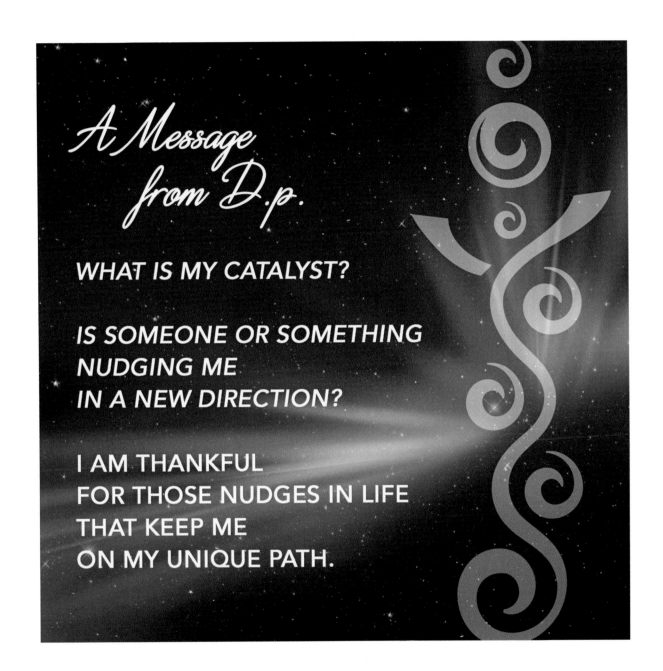

A Message
from D.p.

WHAT IS MY CATALYST?

IS SOMEONE OR SOMETHING
NUDGING ME
IN A NEW DIRECTION?

I AM THANKFUL
FOR THOSE NUDGES IN LIFE
THAT KEEP ME
ON MY UNIQUE PATH.

A Message from D.p.

WHEN I CREATE COHERENCE
BETWEEN THOUGHT & FEELING,

I CREATE CLARITY AND POWER
TO MANIFEST MY DESIRES.

When I try to manifest my desires using only my analytical mind, I am only *thinking* of what I want to create (or, perhaps, what I think I *should* create). But if my feelings are not aligned with those desires, I will remain unbalanced, and my efforts to manifest will be ineffective.

When my thoughts and feelings — my mind and body — are in a state of coherence, I am in alignment with what I want. This inner alignment allows me to manifest with great ease.

PRACTICE: This week, when I think of what I want to manifest, I practice reaching a state of coherence. I do this by staying in the present moment (my body) while thinking my thoughts (my mind) and focusing my awareness on my feelings (my sensations). This alignment brings me clarity and empowers me to manifest my desires with ease.

I can create whatever I want. All I have to do is believe it is possible. I do not need anyone to understand or agree with my creations. And I do not need anyone's permission or approval. I am here for my own evolution, and I understand what I need to do — what I must create — in order to evolve.

PRACTICE: This week, I focus on one experience I wish to create. I remember that in order to do this with ease, I must be in a state of coherence. When I know what I truly desire, I accept it, look within, and create.

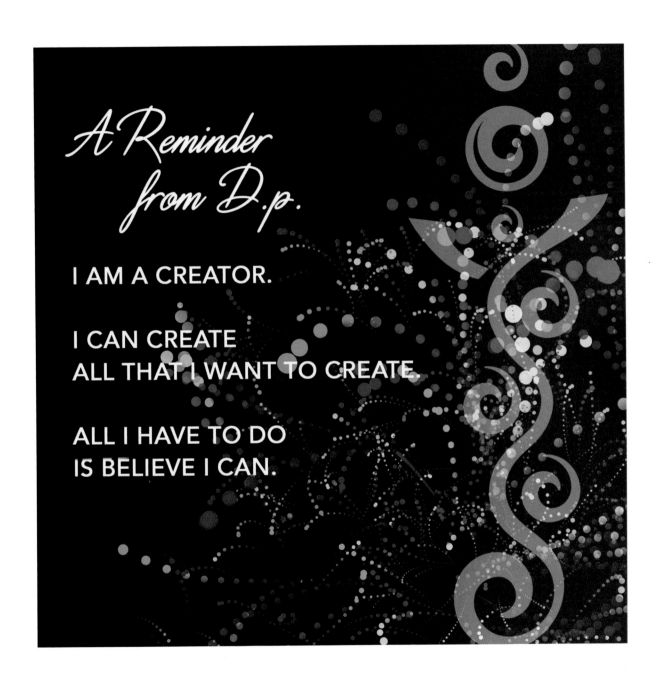

A Reminder
from D.p.

I AM A CREATOR.

I CAN CREATE
ALL THAT I WANT TO CREATE.

ALL I HAVE TO DO
IS BELIEVE I CAN.

— SOURCES —

Becoming Supernatural
by Dr. Joe Dizpensa

Between Death and Life
by Dolores Cannon

Biology of Belief
by Bruce Lipton, PhD

The Convoluted Universe (Books 1–5)
by Dolores Cannon

Energy Speaks
by Lee Harris

Feelings Buried Alive Never Die...
by Karol Truman

Gene Keys
by Richard Rudd

The Hidden Messages in Water
by Masaru Emoto

The Kybalion
by Three Initiates

The Life and Teachings of the Masters of the Far East
by Baird T. Spalding

Molecules of Emotion
by Candace Pert, PhD

The Power of the Subconscious Mind
by Joseph Murphy

The Secret
by Rhonda Byrne

Self-Mastery... A Journey Home to Your Self
by Hu Dalconzo

Storyblocks backgrounds

The Tao Te Ching
by Lao Tzu — translated by John Minford

The Untethered Soul
by Michael A. Singer

What the Bleep Do We Know!?
by William Arntz, Betsy Chasse, Mark Vicente

— GLOSSARY —

The All: everything that exists

Belief: a conscious or subconscious program that creates the reality of my life experience

Conscious Mind: my awareness

Divine (All/Creator/Source): true/eternal all-loving, all-accepting love frequency

D.p.: Divine parent — icon representing eternal all-loving, all-accepting self

Ego (Ego-mind): the subconscious/unconscious programming to protect self

Energy: the fabric of the universe used for creation of matter and non-matter

Fear: an illusion created by the ego

Feeling: a sensation in the body

First Person: thinking and speaking in "me, my," and "I" language so as to create permanent behavioral change by accepting complete responsibility

Free Will: the Divine right of choice that all humans possess

Frequency: a specific vibrational signature of energy

Integrity: being honorable and true

Intention: a thought with feeling that is set forth to create a desired outcome

Intuition: communication from true-self; inner knowing; inner-voice

Law of Attraction (LOA): a universal law that states like vibration attracts like vibration

Love: eternal, unconditional, all-accepting

Power: control, command, dominion, sovereignty

Sensation: a feeling in the body such as pain, tightness, heaviness, heat, tears, numbness, nausea, etc.

True-self: eternal Divine being that knows the truth and purpose of one's experience

Truth: where one's self-harmony resides

— ABOUT THE AUTHOR —

Dr. Sherrilyn Kirchner (Dr. K.) is a metaphysician and owner/founder of Holistic Life Source. Dr. K. works as an online life coach, holistic counselor, and meditation instructor. She offers a self-mastery video series, a D.p. video series, and other enlightening materials on her website: www.holisticlifesource.com.

Dr. K. lives in Indiana with her husband and two children. She dedicates her time to teaching self-mastery techniques through multiple formats to best help her clients holistically evolve into their truest selves.

PHOTO BY JERI HOAG PHOTOGRAPHY

— ACKNOWLEDGMENTS —

I would like to thank my family, friends, and teachers for the amazing support they gave me as I embarked on this journey. While my kids were the original motive for my desire to create a better life, I quickly saw the power of this material, and wanted to share the empowering benefits with others. This is how it became my profession. It has been a challenging endeavor, but well worth every effort. My life experience has benefited greatly from the implementation of this powerful knowledge.

I would like to express my gratitude to my husband and children, who encouraged me to pursue this passion. I would like to especially thank my daughter, Kasey, who helped edit this book and many other Holistic Life Source productions.

— Notes —

— Notes —

— Notes —

Printed in the United States
by Baker & Taylor Publisher Services